God's People at Worship

13 plus

*Young people, worship,
and the all-age church*

Dave Martin

*Jointly published by
Division of Education and Youth
and
Methodist Publishing House*

First published July 1995

© Methodist Church Division of Education and Youth

ISBN 0 7192 0211 6
ISBN 1 85852 048 7

Illustrations: Helen Mahood

Jointly published by
Methodist Church Division of Education and Youth
2 Chester House, Pages Lane, London N10 1PR
and
Methodist Publishing House
20 Ivatt Way, Peterborough PE3 7PG

Printed by
Clifford Frost Limited, Lyon Road,
Windsor Avenue, London SW19 2SE

God's People at Worship

An introduction to the series

'God's People at Worship' is a series of booklets about Christian worship, particularly when all ages are involved.

For simplicity, we use the phrase 'all-age worship' throughout the series, despite its shortcomings. The word 'worship' should need no qualification. In worship, people offer themselves - with all their similarities and differences (including their ages) - to God. Unfortunately, 'worship' is often seen as a mainly adult activity. To describe it as 'all-age' provides a useful reminder that it is the business of the whole people of God.

The booklets in the series deal with different aspects of all-age worship. The emphasis is mainly practical, looking at 'How?' questions. However, 'Why?' questions are also dealt with, particularly in the introductory volume, *One*.

'God's People at Worship' is for worship leaders; for those who plan, prepare and co-ordinate worship in local churches; for workers with children and young people; for church musicians; for people creative in written or spoken word, dance, drama or visual arts; for stewards, members of worship consultations and Church Councils and all who make decisions about the church's worship.

But, above all, we hope that these booklets will be read and used by Christian people of all ages who care about worship.

13 plus, the tenth in the series, looks at young people and worship. What do young people bring to worship and what might they receive? How do they relate to all-age worship? Do they at times need space to 'do their own thing'?

'God's People at Worship' is produced jointly by the Methodist Publishing House and the Division of Education and Youth, in consultation with representatives of the Division of Ministries.

The General Editor of the series is Rev. David Gamble, working with an Advisory Group (Mrs Judy Jarvis, Rev. Peter Barber, Mr Brian Sharp and Mr Brian Thornton).

Thanks

Thanks to all the young people of MAYC who have inspired me in worship and who have made me face some of the tough questions raised in this book. Special thanks to Anthea Cox, Alastair Daniel, Craig McLeish, Anne Richards and Karen Salmon for their technical advice; to Jo Chapman for being the first young person to read the whole book; and to Suzannah England for endless copy corrections.

Dave Martin
July 1995

Contents

1   Introduction

It was Sunday afternoon and Phil was watching TV. Mum stuck her head round the door: 'We're going down to the canal. Are you coming?' 'What, walking?' Mum said nothing else, but Phil heard them all getting ready in the hall. By the time they pulled the front door to, Phil was wondering why he could not have just said: 'OK, good idea'. But sometimes he just liked doing his own thing.

This booklet is aimed at all who lead worship, but particularly those who work with young people, or have a concern about young people's involvement in worship. Perhaps it should have been written by young people, but it is not simply about young people's ideas. It tackles the sometimes confusing issues raised by that period of life often sadly identified as simply a transition from childhood to adulthood. 'Oh, she'll grow out of it.' It tries to take seriously the issues raised by the story of Phil and his Mum. How will the church together create acts of worship that meet the needs of all ages and especially young people? And are there moments when we should encourage young people to develop worship on their own terms and in their own setting?

I hope that the issues raised here will provoke discussion with and among young people. Even more, I hope that the discussion will lead to action and deeper experiences of worship for everyone. There are stacks of ideas to follow, but first let us look at the world of the young person.

2 Young in the Nineties

'Nobody understands me!' is a cry heard in many households. It is often the plea of a teenager. Any serious consideration of worship that involves young people must attempt to understand a little of their complex and changing world.

For most young people in their teens, their whole lifetime has been dominated by only one flavour of politics and for many of them the overriding experience of what life is about is of individualism and materialism. Designer products and much of the high-tech consumer advertising are deliberately targeted at young people (and their parents), underlining the values of success and status in terms of possessions. The rows over designer trainers are a classic example of this.

The education system is under pressure from all sides. Some demand a more efficient and effective system, producing young people fit and ready for business and industry. Others look for academic achievement and schools are being measured accordingly. Young people respond in various ways. One in three young people recently surveyed (Audience Selection survey, *The People,* 4.10.1992) admit that they are staying on in education to see out the economic recession. Four out of ten feel that the system has failed them.

Overall, young people are under pressure to explore their sexuality earlier and many have a confidence that almost shocks their grandparents. The current phrase 'street cred' both highlights the continued growth of youth subcultures, and indicates where many young people gain their knowledge. The open attitude towards sex and drugs that has been breaking all taboos since the 1960s is now no longer confined to the home and private clubs, but is part of public life. The spread of HIV and the subsequent growth of health and sex education programmes means that many young people can discuss sexuality and sexual ethics and practice in a way that even their enlightened parents could not.

The leisure industry has experienced an incredible commercial growth in recent years. Many young people meet in leisure centres, pubs and clubs, or simply on the streets, rather than in youth clubs and centres, uniformed organizations and after-school provision. Some young people spend two to three hours a night in a club or disco and much more at a weekend. This can mean early exposure to drug and alcohol misuse. Recent figures show that 16-24 year-olds spend on average £14 a week on alcohol, with 89% admitting that they had had their first 'proper drink' by the age of 13 (statistics from *The Sheep that got away,* M J Fanstone, 1993).

Television still plays a major role in young people's leisure and entertainment, with the average teenager watching around four hours a day. Evening watershed times for sex and violence mean little to young people who have TV sets in their bedrooms, or whose parents are out working, down the pub, or at church meetings. Alongside the TV, the video and personal computer are, for many young people, their major companions.

At the same time the cycle of deprivation has continued, with the gap between rich and poor growing. Increasing numbers of young people live with unemployment, homelessness, abuse and family breakdown. Many turn to crime out of boredom, for kudos, or to support a drug habit. The fear that once hung over a generation that someone might press a button and start a nuclear war has been replaced by a sense of despair about the ecological destruction of planet earth and the unfairness of the gap between rich and poor. Although some young people certainly take an active interest in these key issues (Amnesty International reported a steady rise in teenage membership in the early 1990s), a general sense of apathy and powerlessness hangs over many more.

One major issue that has probably become more confusing over recent years is the age of maturity. The varying age requirements relating to drivers' licences, drinking alcohol, voting, marriage and homosexual consent, are all in some way indicators both of adulthood and of society's ambivalence about the timing of its emergence. For many, 'adulthood' only really comes with a job, marriage, or financial independence.

Many churches wonder how to respond to this confusing picture. Yet the young have much to offer. Their idealism has not totally disappeared. Some feel helpless, but others are increasingly involved in organizations tackling issues of world poverty, the environment and human rights. Conscious of the multicultural society in which they live, particularly for its influences on music and the surrounding culture, many young people's concerns easily stretch to life in the global village. (Of course, many are also caught up in the serious racial abuse and violence that plagues some communities.) Computers and Information Technology are, for many, part of everyday life. Skills in music and design have been greatly enhanced by such technology and it is young people who are pushing back the boundaries in graphics and software. Many want desperately to be taken seriously for the contribution they can offer.

Having grasped some understanding of the world of a young person, we must guard against lumping them together as a

homogeneous group. The difference in maturity and development between two thirteen-year olds, particularly of different sexes, can be enormous. Their passionate attachment to a particular style of music, clothing, place to meet, or football team varies widely.

We need not attempt to be sociologists, or 'cool', 'cred' youth workers. Simply to try to understand the world of young people in our congregation and in the wider community is a big enough task. For those prepared to listen the rewards are great.

To ask and do, preferably with a cross-section of ages:

- How would you describe the young people
    - in your church?
    - in your community?

- Purchase some teenage magazines and list the key issues addressed in the articles and advertisements.

- Ask a couple of young people what music they prefer and what they get from it.

- What opportunities does your church give to young people to express their needs and concerns and to share their culture?

3 Spirituality

'That was awesome.' For a while in the early 1990s a mainly religious word became very trendy among teenagers. In a sense it was only the next in the succession of fab, hip, wild, ace, cool, wicked, words that described something both very good, and also acceptable to the particular culture of young people. This aspect of the language of culture brings us close to the question of the spirituality of young people.

Young people can be simultaneously both open and questioning, dogmatic and conservative. They are struggling not only with their own identity, but also with their ability to relate feelings and knowledge. It is possible both to know that smoking can kill you and to feel good about being able to smoke. Equally, it is possible to have learnt certain information about God and spirituality and to believe none of it because you are aware that you feel nothing in worship.

For many young people the occasion when they would call something cool, awesome or wicked is when they are dancing, at a concert or sports event, or high on drugs or alcohol. The cynic would say that the rise in popularity of events like Greenbelt, Spring Harvest and even communities like Taizé is simply due to the fact that they exploit young people's need to feel good.

However, it is also clear that expressions of concern about the poverty of worship in this country are related to a general poverty of spirituality. This in turn relates to a generation not used to expressing or handling feelings in private, let alone in public. Spirituality is, of course, more than just getting in touch with feelings, but when young people wish to express what they have understood about God, the world, and themselves,

13

through movement, dance, loud music, or the quiet repetition of a short chorus, some people find it difficult to handle.

Of course, many young people also feel threatened by the outward expression of feelings. Others do not want to conform and resist pressure to do anything. Compare, for example, trying to sing *'Allelu, Allelu, Allelu, Alleluia; Praise ye the Lord!'* (with the stand up and sit down actions) with a group of 7 year-olds, or 30 somethings and with a group of 14 to 15 year olds.

Young people can be especially critical of any hypocrisy they observe in those leading worship, or worshipping with them. They are impatient with those who dislike them clapping in the songs, but insist on chattering during communion. They consider it unfair that a male pony tail, or a purple fringe receive murmurs of disapproval from those wearing a toupee, or a blue rinse. Young people want to see how their faith and spirituality relate to the whole of their lives, their loves and hates, their fears and concerns.

The format, language and content of worship should relate to things that in other contexts feed the minds and lives of young people. Taped contemporary music accompanying prayers and readings can make a significant difference to the atmosphere in the service for a young person. Using an overhead projector for the words of songs and hymns frees them to clap, hold hands with their friends, stand, sit or dance. Informal seating, or a part of the church set aside for those who want to stay on the edge of things, help them feel comfortable.

To do:

- Ask a group of young people to describe occasions when they have felt
  - the world was an amazing place to be;
  - really· calm and peaceful;
  - loved and accepted;
  - the most incredible experience ever.
  (Give permission for, and expect anything!)

- Brainstorm with a group of young people the use of the word 'Lord'. Are any of these uses helpful to us in our understanding of God and Jesus? Is there a contemporary word that would be more usable?

- Find a selection of pictures of Jesus from different eras and different parts of the world. Discuss with the young people which of these help, or hinder in their appreciation of Jesus.

4   Developing Faith

A couple of years ago, I was involved in a youth weekend at which there were workshops to prepare for the evening service in the church. After working with one group on some drama, I left them to develop their ideas on their own and went to visit the others. The group preparing the music and the order of service were already entering numbers next to their order which read: 'hymn, prayer, hymn, reading...........' I returned eventually to the drama group to find them really excited about the idea of bringing in several 'wheelie bins' to the sound of metal dust bin lids being beaten. 'That should really upset a few people!'

Young people can be as rebellious as they are conservative. This applies both to their spiritual development and to the rest of their lives.

In recent years there has been an increasing awareness that we go through a developmental process in our faith journey. Innovative work by Professor James Fowler and others on faith development has been tried and tested in the field of Christian education. Although the 'stages' are not necessarily age-related, it is clear that most of our young people have grown up in church-going families and therefore fall within Fowler's third stage - 'synthetic-conventional' faith.

This is the stage of conforming faith, when what is said by someone a young person respects - whether peers, parents, teachers, or youth group leaders - becomes particularly important. It is a time of going with a particular 'faith-current', or 'faith-crowd' and there may not be much analytical reflection on beliefs and values. Therefore, comments about young people's conservative attitudes are on the one hand a truism about their appropriate stage of faith, but on the other often fall into the trap of criticizing rather than providing the stimulus for broadening their horizons.

In a survey of nearly one thousand church-going adults, Bishop Gavin Reid discovered that 65.2 per cent took significant steps towards faith before they were 13. Though many criticize Church membership classes for their sausage machine mentality and for colluding with peer pressure to 'join', teenage is a significant period for cementing future values and commitments. The challenge facing the church is to make confirmation and membership a highly significant moment for both the church and the young person or adult, without falling into the danger of making it seem an end point.

A related concern is how young people from difficult family backgrounds can discover their role and identity, in particular within the Christian community. The story *Iron John,* by Robert Bly (Dorset: Element Books, 1990) emphasizes through the retelling of an ancient Grimm brothers' story how important it is for a boy to be welcomed into the adult world by men. It has been criticized for being part of a backlash against the feminist movement, but nevertheless raises important questions for the Church about how both young men and young women find appropriate Christian role models.

Regular weekly worship is crucial in the formation of a young person's founding faith, but we must not undervalue the significant role of Junior Church staff and youth group and uniformed organization workers. We must also take particular care over how we mark the rites of passage and other significant moments in our community.

For discussion:

- What opportunities are there during worship for young and old together to share their immediate joys and concerns?

- What opportunities are there for young and/or older people to investigate the claims of Christian faith?

- Are the challenges of Christian commitment and church membership regularly placed before all ages in the church, or just the young?

- Are rites of passage celebrated with enough significance in your church?

- Who are the role models for young women and young men in your church?

5 What are we trying to do?

The young teenage girl climbed the steps of the huge pulpit and, in a slightly over-confident voice, welcomed the congregation to the monthly youth service. She announced the first hymn and stood self-consciously in her pitch pine isolation, whilst her friends clapped gallantly through the slow paced organ accompaniment of *'He sent me to give the Good News to the poor'.* After announcing the drama group's version of the parable of the Great Feast, she rushed, relieved, to the sanctuary of the front pew. As the eighteenth birthday celebration at the front of the church finally filled up with homeless people and concluded with a quick burst of rave music, the congregation burst into applause and another plucky teenager climbed the pulpit steps. After the service I asked the group how they felt it had gone. 'OK,' said some of them, 'but you feel like a performing seal'.

There was no doubting the sincere gratitude of the congregation. They knew they were lucky to have such a committed bunch of young people, were keen to support them and desperate to keep them. However, like the mother asking personal questions about her daughter's latest boyfriend, they were somehow not quite getting it right.

Churches need to ask the same hard question that faces parents: Why do we have children? If it is simply to continue the family name and tradition, or to be an extension of ourselves, or to support us in our old age, we may as parents and as a church be very disappointed. So much of what we do, especially in worship, is often out of a desperation to 'keep' young people and undoubtedly they see right through it. If, in a family, they are quick to point out that it is unfair if not every member has a turn at washing up, or choosing the TV channel, or they are excluded from decisions about where to go on holiday, or what colour to paint the lounge, can we not expect a similar reaction to church and worship? If participation in worship means a monthly (annual!) Youth Service, surely it is no surprise that they are embarrassed at being put on show. If participation means helping to give out the hymn books, but not the bread and wine, it is no surprise that young people call this unfair.

Participation is important for every age group and there are sensitivities that apply to the different aspects of worship. However, this stage of social, physical and spiritual development is important for most teenagers and we ought to put more energy into supporting them, receiving their creativity and listening to their hopes and fears.

To do:

- List all the roles and tasks that exist to make an act of worship.
  Which of these are, or could be, done by young people?

- What other opportunities are there to show that young people's contributions to the life of the church are valued?

6   Together and apart

Every so often the discussion about 'youth church' raises its head. Advocates of 'youth church' suggest that the music styles, language and forms of traditional worship are so far removed from contemporary youth culture that the only option is to scrap it and start again. Opponents suggest that this is divisive and that we should strive to find common ground for all-age worship.

This is not an either-or debate. Both should be possible. For the same reason that all ages in a family have meals, go on holiday, watch sport, go swimming, or make a snowman together, so worship can be an occasion for all ages to contribute and receive. All ages can learn from each other's experience, but equally young people need opportunities to observe how adults and their peers make use of their experience. Most important, young people need opportunities to participate in and learn from the traditions of the faith community in which they are growing up.

Equally, just as young people need their own space to play together and learn from each other, to enjoy their own music and create their own ways of doing things, so too there should be some opportunities for young people to be apart for worship. Many other groups within the church have their own separate acts of worship. Whatever we think of it, commerce and the media have created a huge teenage subculture (several in fact). Connect with this the influence of the peer group and there is clearly a terrific amount of energy and creativity which could be used for the glory of God in worship, but which, for all sorts of reasons, may not emerge in an all-age gathering. There are new movements in all areas of society which have only come about because a group of people (often the young) have been free to experiment released from traditions, prejudices and assumptions.

Many young people have grown up in a totally unchurched background and for them the environment, concepts and music styles of most traditional worship is totally alien. Young people in our congregations may need a more culturally friendly environment for worship to which they will feel comfortable inviting their friends.

Examples are given later of some of the radical attempts to renew worship according to patterns of youth culture. It is worth noting, however, that in many instances where these developments have taken place, the age group of those attending quickly expands and the overall worship life of the church is quickly enriched.

Idea:

- Many churches and/or circuits have a youth service created by young people meeting together during the Sunday afternoon for workshops.

- In other places, these workshops are all-age, with young people either leading or co-leading, contributing skills and ideas.

- Why not try both models?

7 Widening horizons

Whether together or apart, the issue of how young people are empowered to feel part of and contribute to all-age worship is crucial. Young people hate being patronized. Most want to be stretched and challenged. The key is to find ways of broadening horizons and giving a taste of what is possible and then supporting the young people in evaluating this experience without imposing our own preconceptions and prejudices.

Many young people experience a whole variety of styles of worship at the big Christian festivals. MAYC London Weekend tries to include various styles in one service; Easter People usually has several different venues catering for different traditions; Greenbelt probably gives the most immediate access to a number of the major new styles of worship. Group or church leaders sometimes find such events and their lively worship threatening. Very often because of size, technology and available skills, it simply is not repeatable, but rather than just spending the following weeks scraping the young people off the ceiling, it should be possible to help them to evaluate what is was beyond the atmosphere that they would identify as important elements of worship.

Idea:

- A small group of adults could join the Junior Church and/or Youth Group in visiting other denominations or events to see what is different, or to learn about 'their' worship. They could also ask more searching questions about what worship is and whether any aspects of what has been experienced could be used in the local situation.

At local level young people need opportunities to experience the different aspects of worship. We often ask individual young people to read a lesson, say a prayer, or give out the hymn books, but there are many other roles which young people rarely have access to, often because there is a feeling that these are the things you do if you are going to take it on 'seriously'.

The Organ: I can remember the one church where I recently saw a young person playing as the congregation arrived. She played one hymn during the service, the resident organist doing the rest. Talking to her afterwards, she had no designs on taking over, but the organist had heard her express an interest and had encouraged her to play a little every now and then.

Communion: When young people have taken part in the prayers and distribution of the elements, there have often been comments from adults about how moving it is to receive from them.

Local Preachers: Working with a preacher need not always be to test a call, but may often be a way that young people feel that they can 'do' something. Particularly in rural areas, a small group of young people accompanying a local preacher to sing, act or read, will often be received enthusiastically.

Other areas where young people can contribute skills and creativity alongside all ages include choirs, music groups, banner making, flower arranging and other decorations, drama and dance groups. The only reasons for not including them fully in the life of the church are a proper concern about homework and their own social life.

8 Signs, symbols and plenty of hugs

Symbolism is very powerful in youth culture and is often connected to the tribalism of the subcultures. Wearing Dr Marten's, or wedges, or a certain brand of trainers, symbolizes allegiance to a certain group, or fashion trend. The symbols we use in worship are also important. They need to reflect the Kingdom and point to Christ.

Most churches are now much happier about using crosses, candles, banners and other aids to worship and meditation. Too frequently, however, the symbols are placed in the worship and spoken about, or simply left to speak for themselves, rather than used specifically in some aspect of the worship. During communion, to take time to handle the bread and feel its texture before eating, or to pass around a candle during intercessory prayers, is to allow the symbols to evoke their own meaning. Handling real nails during a reading of the Passion and Crucifixion, feeling seeds and corn during the parable of the Sower, or barbecuing sardines on Easter Monday morning all add life and imagination to familiar stories.

Recognizing that young people are easily embarrassed and that they have very fertile imaginations is also a vital ingredient to the way signs, symbols and actions are handled. Handing out uninflated balloons may soon get some giggling, but equally there may be some less obvious surprises, so always check first. Sensitive introductions and a not too intense approach can also lead to symbols and actions releasing great creativity and giving the more shy and retiring the permission they need to join in. Passing round symbols can release smiles, eye contact and touch between the ages and bridge gaps that words have not.

Incense and perfumed oils, though frowned on by some for their association with the New Age movement, can be very evocative when used with appropriate readings from Scripture. (Note: you may need to check for any asthma sufferers.) Perfumed oils can also be used simply for rubbing a drop on the palm of a neighbour's hand as a sign of fellowship, to bless one another with a cross on the forehead, or as an active sign when praying for healing.

Pictures have been a vital part of Christian worship for many centuries. Protestant, Free Church worship has probably been the most resistant to the revival of interest in art and pictures both as 'background' and focus of worship. Next to music, visual images are probably the most important influence on the development of youth culture. Moving video images are an obvious place to start, but we need to remember that much of today's graphic design is generated by young people. It is not always necessary to go for complex video arrangements. Slide and overhead projectors can produce good quality images. Black-out does not need to be total, but sunlight can easily destroy the effectiveness of projection. Project as large an image as possible. A good, large, clean sheet gives an excellent image for a backdrop. Screens are probably best used when asking a congregation to meditate, or focus on an image. Cross fading with several projectors is very effective, but requires good equipment and rehearsal. Many photographic outlets will hire this equipment, but schools and local authorities may be willing to lend or hire to a youth group, especially one registered with the authority.

The cross, of course, is the most evocative and powerful of all symbols. Perhaps because it is used so widely in jewellery, fashion and many art forms, it needs handling with care and sensitivity, so that young people can really personalize its worth for them. The way a cross is represented, in rough wood, or ornate brass, where it is placed and how it is used will speak volumes about our view of its centrality to the Christian Gospel. Placing written prayers, or candles, or emptying pockets or school bags at the foot of the cross can symbolize handing over to Jesus. Placing small crosses on a world or local map, or on a selection of newspaper cuttings or photographs can symbolize our desire to see Jesus working and healing in these situations. Without using words, young and old together can come to appreciate each others' concerns, depths of spirituality and need for God.

Having tried **foot washing** several times with youth groups, it is probably one of the most unpredictable of symbolic actions. A group that had been riotous all weekend carried it out with great meaning and seriousness, whereas a previously intense group of students just tickled each other mercilessly. However, I have found nothing more profoundly moving than an all-age group washing each other's feet. Hand washing is a less embarrassing alternative.

Not all teenagers are as huggable and hugging as the annual green and yellow invasion of London would imply. However, with sensitive introduction, giving permission for more than the conventional wet fish handshake during **The Peace** can be very affirming for all ages. When connected with the forgiveness and reconciliation which it symbolizes, it can quickly lead to the restoration of friend, family and community relationships.

One way of formalizing the end of a conference or important act of worship is for one person, not necessarily the preacher or leader, to stand at the exit. The second person greets him/her and then stands alongside them. The next person then greets the first person, then the second and stands alongside them. An ever expanding wedding reception queue is created, where everyone gets a chance to greet everyone else. With more than about thirty people two queues may be necessary. Singing something appropriate for the mood of the occasion can also help. *(Let there be love shared among us; Alle Alle Alle; We are marching in the light of God.)*

The importance of non-embarrassing, informal moments for some personal touch, or word of thanks, forgiveness, or farewell cannot be overstated. They are also moments open to the working of God's Spirit. Young people are very quick to take up opportunities for meaningful response or action, so long as it is not forced on them, or does not lead to some major action that draws direct attention to them. Only the most dreadfully manipulative, or spiritually gifted evangelist will do an 'altar call' with young people. Often in a communion service at the close of a youth, or all-age church weekend, rather than have a formal distribution of the elements, I have

left the table with enough bread and cups of wine for anyone to come and serve any other person as they see fit. It provides an opportunity to tie up any loose ends in relationships, say sorry, or thank you, pray for healing, or simply say goodbye. Some background music can be helpful, because the end of the music also signifies the end of what will inevitably be a lot of movement.

9 Presenting the Word

'Sermons are boring.' The constant plea I hear from young people preparing worship, whether for youth services, weekends, conferences, consultations or for MAYC London Weekend in the Royal Albert Hall is: 'No sermon. We do not want some boring old fogey telling us what to believe.' Well, I have tried not to take it personally. I agree with the sentiment, apart perhaps from the 'old fogey' bit. Young people, like the rest of us, want to be taken seriously when God's word is being presented. It only becomes boring if it seems to have nothing to do with my everyday experience, or if it is presented in a way that is totally unintelligible to me. If the message about Jesus is Good News, then I want to be told how and why and not simply that I must believe that it is so.

Young people's negative reaction to sermons is not surprising when you consider the ways in which they normally receive information, at school and on TV. Even in the most traditional of education establishments, the amount of time teachers spend delivering their message from the chalk face is fairly limited and is usually accompanied by plenty of board writing and drawing, maps, diagrams and plastic replicas of the backbone of the *tridendipoflarbrunsaurus.* As for TV, words plus music plus pictures only scratch the surface of the impact many programmes have on the brain. Try only listening to or only watching a modern cartoon (and I do not mean *Tom and Jerry*), or counting the seconds that any one image remains on your screen during a programme like the *Clothes Show* and you will see what I mean. Young people are used to receiving information in bite sized chunks and accompanied by at least one other media form.

Drama

Two other volumes in this series (*Drama* and *Story*) explore mime, drama, movement and choral reading as ways into the Bible and the sermon. These methods have long been advocated, but are still rarely attempted. They can be particularly important for young people.

Young people need to be able to laugh and shout. They need to be able to laugh at themselves and poke fun at aspects of the Church which they are trying to understand. They also need to be able to shout about some of the serious issues, which they may only partly understand, or others that affect them directly. Drama and movement allow them to express things that they would probably not otherwise be able to put into words.

Young people also need to be able to experiment with the ideas and feelings that are all part of being a teenager and developing in faith. For a drama or movement contribution truly to enable young people to express these ideas and feelings and to communicate them to other people, they need to have a sense of control over what they are doing. If someone (usually the group leader) brings in a ready-made script, the overall focus can easily switch from experimenting, discovering and expressing to performing. Some material produced by Christian theatre companies, or the popular Wild Goose scripts are very clever and witty and relevant to contemporary experience. However, a group left to their own devices, or helped to work on things that concern them, may not be as slick, but will certainly produce something more genuine and faces will not be lost in mountains of (illegally) photocopied sheets.

I worked once with a group on the story of Jesus stilling the storm. We talked about times when we feel afraid. To begin with there was plenty of discussion about our various phobias and then one of the girls said that the time when she really felt afraid was when her parents went out for the evening and she was left alone. We began to act it out and the humour came as her 'parents' left for a Church Council meeting. The group had difficulty in thinking what it would mean for Jesus to come and 'still the storm' in this situation, since although she might overcome fantasies about the dark or a dripping tap, recent incidents locally gave every reason for being concerned about burglary, or rape. Although none of us was particularly happy with the ending to the scene, the arrival of a friend and their sharing of their fears and need to trust God gave it a reality, which needed little further explanation from the preacher.

It is easy to force young people into presenting their ideas and feelings in a way that is alien to them and therefore off-putting. Witty church sketches and liturgical dance are a genre all of their own and are very different from youth culture. Young people often have very strong preferences about their own culture and they will use aspects of it to express what is really important to them.

Movement

The use of dance in worship is still at a very embarrassed and embarrassing stage. First, it is usually interpretive, which means that for the untrained and unskilled, there are only just so many hand, arm and leg movements that can be used to interpret a Graham Kendrick chorus, or the latest chart topping love song. Second, since most of the boys would not be seen dead scooping themselves around the communion area, asking young girls to dress in leotards and bits of chiffon only reinforces a certain image of liturgical dance. Which brings me to one of the reasons why boys will often not join in. Any lad who has the courage to get on the dance floor at a disco usually does so for two reasons. First because he has rhythm and loves his body to respond to the beat or, second, to display his growing awareness of his sexual prowess.

Using dance in worship with young people needs to allow more for development of expressions of praise, adoration, confession and worship, rather than specific interpretation. If a particular message or interpretation is to be conveyed, then the movements need to be explored first and only then appropriate music found. If soft, gentle music is chosen, the movement still needs to be strong and clear in its design. Flowing movements are not the same as 'floaty' movements. The former is elegant and evocative, the latter, limp and unconvincing.

We also need to create a secure and supportive environment for young people to explore movement and the use of their bodies. Care needs to be taken over what to wear. When costumes are allowed to happen without discussion they can range from the indecent to jeans and heavy jumpers. We can use a whole range of styles of music, but we particularly need to be bold in including contemporary rhythms and beat, thus allowing young people room for some really energetic expression. When choreographing to this type of music, young people are guided more by the power and rhythm than by any words. As a result, the movements are more elastic and versatile and flow more naturally from the dancers' bodies and the piece is more engaging to watch.

Ideas:

- **Theatre Games** These help individuals participate in a group in a non-threatening way and build up the group relationships. Trust games are probably the best-known example, such as allowing yourself to fall, stiff bodied, backwards into another person's arms. Another idea is for each person to invent an action that describes them and then to introduce themselves by the action to another person. An extension of this is to teach the second person how to perform the action by moving their arms, hands, mouth, etc., appropriately.

- **Improvisation** Helps to imagine and experience being different people in all sorts of circumstances. Since no script is required, everyone has a chance to contribute ideas freely and naturally. Small groups of three or four can imagine they are at a fairground facing one of the really scary rides. One of the group is asked to act as though they are petrified and the rest of the group try to persuade them to join in.

- **Chanted improvisation** A group of voices chanting odd words or phrases can be very effective in creating an atmosphere. The choice of words, the pitch, volume and stress of the voice all contribute to the differing effects.

- **Masks** These enhance the portrayal of a character and are a support for weaker acting skills. The audience latch on to the character more quickly. Plain masks can be very effective in creating a 'unified' appearance, or in enhancing movement, as opposed to voice or facial expression. They are also useful in depersonalizing roles and characters.

- **Role play** Issues, or situations that make young people feel uncomfortable in real life, can be discussed and explored in role play. The characters and plot can be imposed on the group, or developed by the group themselves. Exploring the characters and reviewing the process are the vital elements to role play, but an edited version of the end product often makes excellent drama for worship.

- **Mime** Only eight per cent of normal communication is verbal. The key purpose of mime is to achieve maximum communication with minimum words. Mime does not have to be in total silence. The use of a single word can be very effective. Every movement carries particular significance and, in mime, space is treated as an object and the movements bring it to life. A story can be told in this imaginary world to great effect. To warm up, hand out cards with a 'space' to move within - supermarket, church, office, classroom. Participants are asked not to make obvious gestures, e.g., crossing self in church - but to move around their space.

- **_Physical theatre_** Bridges the traditional gap between drama and dance. There is a large amount of contact between participants and ideas are represented using the body rather than words. Its use can increase the intensity of drama work, especially when the body is used in innovative ways. An exploration of Jesus and the cross could lead to one person carrying another on his/her back like a cloak, or burden. The person being carried could then try representing a cross, or sin.

A further idea would be to look at Jesus turning the tables in the Temple. The group talks through the actions of falling and tumbling, and warms up by pushing each other over and practising rolling over. Then they leapfrog over each other, or in pairs, link arms back to back and lift each other up. Using a firefighter's lift, or some other, individuals can be passed from group to group. Martial Arts style moves can be very effective, such as a high kick towards a line of people, who then fall like a wall collapsing.

- **_Building movement_** Is a way of starting with groups that have little confidence in dance and concentrates on what the participants can achieve, rather than a polished performance. Each individual is asked to experiment for a while to find a gesture or movement which they like and can easily repeat. Each person then teaches their movement to another, and the pair to another pair, until a group of four has learned four movements. The groups are then asked to put the four movements together in an order that they feel flows well. The person working with the group now makes a swift decision about what piece of music, or reading would best suit the kinds of movements being created. Together, the small groups should be encouraged to find an order to fit each set of movements that begins to 'match' the feel of the music, or reading. The group that has not experienced dance before will often be amazed by the result. Others could probably develop something more creative, having gained confidence this far.

It is vital to give enough time for experimentation and discussion. Where role play or masks are being used, debriefing is crucial, since entering into the experience of another person can deeply affect feelings and emotions. Young people need to feel comfortable about what they, individually and as a group, are doing and to be confident that the piece expresses what they want to communicate.

As many preachers discover, what you think you have said will be interpreted in different ways by the listeners and what you thought was clear as day when pen hit paper may stay locked in the dark mystery of communication when it crosses the front aisle. So it is with those who use drama and dance in worship, especially when it is wrapped in the clothing of the subcultures of the 1990s. Some will find its interpretation very difficult, but others will find their understanding of the Gospel greatly enriched.

Testimony

The use of personal testimonies, especially by young people in all-age worship, can be a very effective way of bringing live experience in support of the sermon. Obviously, these need careful preparation. The super confident, effervescent teenager, who has just made a personal and significant commitment to Christ at a mission, or other event, may become a real turn off by their attitude or simply by talking for too long. Equally, their freshness, plain talking and obvious love for Jesus have the power to touch the hearts of every age group. The emphasis should be on personal stories that are real and up to date. Expect stories of dramatic conversion, but also look for everyday examples of 'What Jesus means to me now' and 'How I have recognized God with me this week'. Look too for the 'hard' examples of struggle and pain so that, again, all ages can share in the realities of each other's journeys.

A few years ago, at the final celebration in the Easter People young people's meetings, there was an open invitation for anyone to come and say what God had done for them during the week. I feared either total silence, or a queue of increasingly dramatic conversion stories. Instead, a stream of teenagers came to the microphone and, in a few sentences, simply spoke of their increased love for God, how a relationship had been sorted out, some real meaning to life found, a call to the ministry felt, and so it continued. A number finished with: 'So, if you haven't found Jesus yet, give him a go.' Pure Gospel. I did not need to preach. They had spoken to their peers in a way that I could not.

10 Music

Grunge, garage, gangster, funk, house, indie, metal, techno, progressive, bungra, hip hop, rap, rock, rave, reggae, ragga, jungle, not to mention NWA...... just scratching the surface of the contemporary music scene in names alone. Of course, many young people are just as keen on classics and the modern composers. Music is still one of the prime movers in youth culture and needs to be taken seriously in any worship that seeks to involve and include them. There are a few assumptions, however, that need to be addressed.

First, not all young people want to sing seven Graham Kendrick choruses in every service. However, a lively beat is so important to most contemporary music that, in comparison, singing hymns that constantly refuse to include more than the odd quaver and whose base line is harmonious rather than driving can seem positively sleepy.

Second, not all modern music has to be deafeningly loud. It does have to be loud enough to lead the singing, but quality and clarity are crucial to the musical ear of the 1990s. CD players, in-ear stereo headphones, keyboards with sequencers, all mean that most of us now have access to excellent quality reproduction. Sadly, many churches still invest very little in even the PA system for the preachers, let alone any further amplification for instruments, or prerecorded music.

Third, the appearance of a guitar does not mean young people will come clamouring into worship. Many, especially those into rock and metal music, like to see the skilled guitarist fronting a band. However, most of the music genres described above are dominated by the keyboard and the sequencer. Piano is still the most popular (or at least most played) instrument by children and young people, hence the immediate interest in keyboards and all they can now achieve. Junior schools usually teach recorder first, which means that the flute is the most frequent next choice for many children. The 'trendy' instrument of the late 1990s is probably the saxophone.

Use of instruments and simple arrangements

Any keen instrumentalists should not be excluded from having a go! It is possible to blend together effectively instrumentalists of all kinds and abilities. Advanced instrumentalists may be given the music and then improvise an arrangement, which can be very creative. Less advanced instrumentalists probably need parts specifically written for them. A good sound can be produced from a group of the least experienced if plenty of time is invested in practising, both to get it right and to build up their confidence.

When to use instruments:

Before worship to create the atmosphere.

As a quiet background to prayer and meditation or to a Bible reading.

Working with the organist to accompany the singing of hymns and worship songs. (Experiment with which instruments give the most appropriate accompaniment to which songs. Some worship songs are better played on instruments other than the organ.)

Ways to use specific instruments:

Piano or keyboard: often the basis of an instrumental group, giving a strong lead for other instruments. Try to utilize the different sounds and textures fully, e.g., a string pad to back a quieter song. (If two keyboards are available, use one as a piano sound and the other to provide other textures - strings, brass, as solo instruments.) Many modern keyboards have sequencers built in, which enable you to play music into the keyboard and record it before worship, e.g., it is possible to put in the chords and bass and then improvise over it live. Also most keyboards now have a modulation facility which enables you to find a singable key if a particular piece of music is pitched extremely high or low.

Guitars: can be played in some hymns but are generally more effective in worship songs providing harmony and rhythm. If you have more than one guitarist, one could play chords, another take the role of lead guitar and another the bass line.

Melody Instruments: including flutes, recorders, oboes, violins and clarinets can be used for the melody or for a descant or another harmony line. Often more advanced players can improvise a counter-melody.

Brass Instruments: can be used as solo instruments, but are often more effective in worship songs when used in blocks together as 'fills' in between the melody to add a new dimension to the overall texture of the music.

Cellos, trombones and euphoniums: these are great for the bass or the tenor line. If you have to choose between the tenor and bass, go for bass - the tenor harmonies could be filled in elsewhere, even in a different octave.

Percussion: both drumkits and other percussion instruments can be used effectively in worship - not just in the lively songs either. Many songs and hymns benefit from the percussion textures being added sensitively. Drum machines can be used, but need careful programming in order to sound good and they do not leave much room for flexibility and variety.

Where to get arrangements

Hymns and Psalms is available from the Methodist Publishing House.

Songs of Fellowship (Instrumental and Vocal), PRO Box 4, Sheffield S1 1DU.

Carol Praise Marshall, Morgan & Scott/Harper and Collins.

Hymns for the People. (Keyboard arrangements by David Peacock) Harper and Collins.

Music from Taizé Volumes 1 & 2. (Instrumental and Vocal) Collins.

Simple keyboard arrangements

The Complete Praise Keyboard Player by Paul Douglas and Dean Austin, PO Box 15, Nottingham NG6 9JZ (there is also a version for the piano).

Using unaccompanied songs

There is some excellent material from all around the world. Many songs are most effective in four-part harmony and have parts that are quite simple, but need to be well taught. One way is simply by repetition by ear as gradually people become familiar with their part. If you have a group who can read music then it should be quite easy to learn new songs. If the song is in a foreign language sometimes it is easier to learn the music first perhaps to vowel sounds and then learn the words after.

Resources:
> *Freedom is coming* Protest and Praise from South Africa Wild Goose Publications
> *Sent by the Lord* Wild Goose Publications
> *Songs of the World Church* Wild Goose Publications
> *Dance on Injustice* Greenbelt Festivals
> *Many and Great* Wild Goose Publications
> *Sing Freedom* Songs from South Africa Christian Aid and Novello
> *World Praise* Marshall Pickering/Harper Collins

Using Backing Tracks

Backing tracks can be useful in churches where there are no other instruments. *Hymns and Psalms* is now available on CD, but is very expensive for a full set. The Spring Harvest 94 Song-book has a tape backing track. Obviously, these reduce the flexibility for a congregation to repeat things or to stop for a prayer, but with new music, if the church organist is not at ease playing it, and there are no other instrumentalists, it might be the best option.

Other uses of music

Music is very powerful and emotive. Listening to the TV without watching will give a clue to just how much it is used in every kind of programme to support the visual images and the spoken word. Music conjures up deep feelings in us, evokes all kinds of images and can make contact with memories and past experiences. David's harp playing soothed Saul's troubled spirit. Therefore, music to accompany readings, prayers, drama, or movement, or even to act as a link should be chosen with care and sensitivity. I can remember a service where a dramatic portrayal of Abraham's virtual sacrifice of Isaac was accompanied by Pavarotti singing a Puccini aria. The emotion was almost unbearable. Having said that, since music has that great capacity to help us make that long journey from the head to the heart, we should be prepared sometimes for tears and allow old and young quietly to comfort each other.

There are other matters to consider when using music. First, always hear the piece all the way through, to ensure it is long enough for the purpose and to check for any hidden surprises (faults on the tape or disk, or inappropriate 'noises off'). I once used the track *Sadness* by Enigma while people wrote prayers of intercession. It starts with an almost Gregorian chant and then breaks into a slow dance beat. About two-thirds of the way through there is a sudden break for some feminine heavy breathing! Fortunately most people were too engrossed in their praying to notice as I dived for the volume control.

Second, if the music is intended to support another part of the service, then the volume needs to be controllable and from a suitable place. Sound mixing should ideally take place centrally, at the back of the congregation but forward of any balcony or overhang. If this cannot happen, someone sitting in this area should assist with hand signals. If the church has a loop induction system always try to guarantee that additional amplification is connected to it.

Third, rehearsal is vital. Those who lead any singing need to be clear about introductions, especially if mainly guitars are being used. Short and obvious lead-ins are most helpful to congregations. Rehearsing a song's ending is just as important. (Do not forget to count the verses!) Scrappy endings, especially where last lines or last bars are repeated, can be very annoying. Being clear here means that openness to repeating a verse or chorus becomes much less worrying. Links with taped or live music also need rehearsing, so that the flow supports the move from one part of the service to the next.

Finally, although involving young people in this aspect of worship is crucial, and many will find great expression of their spirituality through playing or singing, getting too caught up in the practical and technical arrangement may be more of a distraction than a help.

Copyright warning!

The issue of Copyright is fraught with difficulty. Basically, if you are using something that has been produced by somebody else, you should seek their permission. This means, for example, that, unless permission has been given by the authors, drama scripts should not be photocopied, even for rehearsal.

As far as prerecorded music is concerned, an act of worship is considered a public performance and therefore permission is needed. Any copying of words or music of songs, or hymns less than seventy years old is also not allowed without permission, or a licence. A licence to reproduce certain songs can be obtained from Christian Copyright Licensing, PO Box 1339, Eastbourne BN21 4YF (Tel: 01323 417711, Fax: 01625 524510). Some music publishers produce their own acetates of words, which may be used without a licence. Detailed guidance is contained in *To copy, or not to copy - that is the question,* and in *Worth Doing Well,* available from the Methodist Publishing House.

11   Ambience - Sound - Light

One temptation facing all who enter this technical arena is the desire to bring out every piece of equipment at once. It is important first to decide what will provide the atmosphere that is relevant and conducive to worship in the particular setting. Second, the time, people involved and cost need to be balanced against the end product.

Ideas:

- Project pertinent images on to walls and screens, helping to create an atmosphere and to draw the attention of the congregation to something specific.

- Use computer sequencing packages to control keyboards and samplers. This can be used to create music live and before the worship.

- There are also computer packages that will produce words and images which can be superimposed on to video. Microsoft Powerpoint is very useful, though expensive. Corelshow is easier to use and cheaper. You will need a Genlock to create this effect. Computers can also be used in preparation for worship, preparing the music, slides, editing video, and controlling lighting.

TV and video can be used effectively in worship. Monitors can be linked together so that everyone can easily see one. There is opportunity here to use many different images by including home shot material of the locality, or prerecorded clips from the news, wild life programmes, films, or adverts. These can be used to portray a specific message, support prayers or readings, or to create an atmosphere.

Good lighting helps to create the right atmosphere. Again, it is not essential to have a full rock concert lighting rig, but to recognize the key role that lighting plays in youth subculture. It should create an atmosphere of informality whilst still arousing a sense of awe and expectancy that something special is going to happen. Single spotlights can be very effective in highlighting a solo contribution, but this should be well rehearsed to find the right size for the spot and to be sure the person stands in the correct place and is used to the stark contrasts of light and dark.

Good use of all amplification is also crucial, especially as it will often be in connection with a variety of other pieces of equipment, live instrumentalists and singers. The sound needs to be powerful but not painfully loud. PA can be hired, borrowed, made or bought. Groups should be encouraged to raise money, but Church Councils also need to offer appropriate support.

Whatever you try to do, make sure the young people are involved right from the outset. Often they know a lot more about the technical side than the adults they are working with. We need to learn to trust them to use their skills more fully in order to create worship which is relevant to them. As technology moves on, new developments should be observed carefully for new applications in worship. Currently 'multimedia' appears to be the buzzword, but obviously this will develop with time and it is most likely that the young people will be the first to spot the new ideas.

12 Worship and Outreach

Worship at its best brings the worshipper to a real sense of the presence of God. 1 Corinthians 14:24 suggests that an unbeliever should be able to walk in on our worship and say: 'God is really among you!' A culture gap exists for many young people between what they experience in most church worship and any other event which communicates using words, music and symbolism. Whilst the Church needs to develop its own cultural forms, if we are to reach young people who have no previous experience of church life and worship, we have to try to bridge the gap.

Many young people's first contact with the church will be through a youth group, or uniformed organization, or particular project. They may be introduced to worship within the group setting and eventually through the drip feeding of youth services and family services to more frequent contact with the regular worship. However, some would argue that this is totally patronizing and constantly squeezes out any innovations, or gifts that these young people bring to the community. For the purposes of outreach to unchurched young people, but also for the creative renewal of our worship, there is an argument for separate young people's worship.

There are now many examples around the country where worship is being constructed by and for young people, with a particular emphasis on youth subculture. Often it has a specifically evangelistic purpose. However, this is not always the case and some groups have not only broken with tradition, but also with orthodoxy and they raise a different set of questions that cannot be tackled within the confines of this book.

What has now received the umbrella title of 'Alternative Worship', started in most instances not as an attempt to mimic a particular piece of youth subculture, but as a genuine attempt by those working with young people to help them to express in their own forms what they most wanted to say about God, to God, and to hear from God. This developmental stage seems a crucial element to most of the major projects which have attempted something like this.

Since youth culture is so diverse and rapidly changing, any attempt to create alternative worship styles should be worked out in the local context. A good youth worker and a key group of young people is, of course, essential. A basic question might be: 'What form and content would you give to worship to be comfortable bringing your friends to it?' It may be that if the church runs an open youth club, the question of what could be done to help them express their hopes, fears, concerns and beliefs might not only open up fascinating discussion, but also lead to some amazingly meaningful moments.

Where this has been tried, first attempts are often more like an evening of favourite dance tracks accompanied by a collage of gruesome newspaper headlines, than a recognizable act of worship. However, it expresses the needs and feelings of the young people using the tools available, and that initially is important.

As things develop, it is important to enable some of the more adventurous ideas actually to happen, e.g., linking up a number of TV sets so that a music video can have more impact, even hiring a video projector. You could use the club's disco deck to link several pieces of music together, to dance to a track whilst watching slides or a video about issues that concern the group, or images that they feel describe what, or who God is. Remember the importance of young people actually handling the equipment.

How things progress will depend on the nature of the group. If the majority are well in tune with Christianity and what worship is about, then the concepts may move on rapidly, although stereotypes and preconceptions may be harder to overcome. If some of the group have little idea about Christianity, which is probably the ideal, the interaction of ideas, forms, concepts and beliefs will be crucial to the development, and the worker will have a significant role. Outrageous suggestions will be vetoed by the group, if handled well. Discussion about whether particular words or music are appropriate should lead to growth in understanding both of faith and of worship. How, for example, would you react to the use of the Lenny Kravitz song *Believe* which includes both the words: 'The Son of God is in our face, offering us eternal grace...' and 'I am you and you are me . . . you just gotta believe in yourself'?

In the places where this concept has really taken off in recent years, two movements can be detected. The first is where the whole 'event' has become so sophisticated and technically orientated, that it has, of necessity, involved more and more able and skilled and older people. What often started out with middle to late teens, has often become a sophisticated community of twenty and thirty somethings. From these groups some serious and challenging questions about the development of liturgy are beginning to emerge. The second movement is where, partly again because of technical sophistication and partly because of the large numbers being attracted, these acts of worship have turned into large scale events on a monthly, or less frequent basis with a number of fringe happenings and often 'guest' speakers. They often provide a glimpse of the possible for young people, and ideas, inspiration and resources for youth workers.

It is vitally important to keep going back to the original question about what we are trying to achieve. At local level, where things are usually done on a small scale, we have the advantage of keeping relationships personal, building something that works and, most crucially, builds young people with their growing faith commitment into the all-age community.

Resources

Youth Culture and the Gospel   Pete Ward   Marshall Pickering

Worship and Youth Culture   Pete Ward   Marshall Pickering

Outside In   Mike Breen   Scripture Union

Teenage Beliefs   Day/May   Lion Publishing

Fast Moving Currents in Youth Culture   Lynx

Rave On, a worship guide for youth groups   Simon Heathfield   Church Pastoral Aid Society

The Iona Community Worship Book   Wild Goose Publishing

Wild Goose Songs Vols 1-4   Wild Goose Publishing

Let's Praise 1 and 2   Marshall Pickering

The Dame Cecily Spume Drama Note Book   Nick Page Monarch

Much Ado about Something   Andrew Smith   CPAS

Much Ado about Something Else   Andrew Smith   CPAS

The Late Late Service   9 Woodlands Road, Glasgow G4 9EQ

Regenerate Magazine   Greenbelt Festivals

MAYC staff are available to offer advice, technical help, information and workshops on any of the issues mentioned in this book.